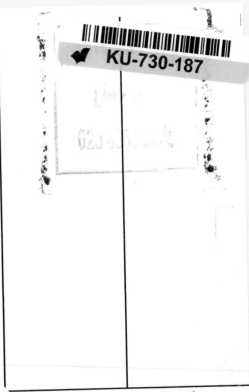

n/renew this item by the
vn to avoid a charge.
he renewed by phone
not be renewed if
ther reader.

arnet.gov.uk

NET
DON BOROUGH

©Published 2022.
BookLife Publishing Ltd.
King's Lynn, Norfolk PE30 4LS

ISBN 978-1-80155-144-1

All rights reserved. Printed in Poland.
A catalogue record for this book is available
from the British Library.

Rock Bottom
Written by William Anthony
Illustrated by Drue Rintoul

An Introduction to Accessible Readers...

Our 'really readable' Accessible Readers have been specifically created to support the reading development of young readers with learning differences, such as dyslexia.

Our aim is to share our love of books with children, providing the same learning and developmental opportunities to every child.

INCREASED FONT SIZE AND SPACING improves readability and ensures text feels much less crowded.

OFF-WHITE BACKGROUNDS ON MATTE PAPER improves text contrast and avoids dazzling readers.

SIMPLIFIED PAGE LAYOUT reduces distractions and aids concentration.

CAREFULLY CRAFTED along guidelines set out in the British Dyslexia Association's Dyslexia-Friendly Style Guide.

Rock Bottom

Written by William Anthony

Illustrated by Drue Rintoul

Chapter One:
From Top to Bottom

"Phil, please. We need you to take this job," begged Whittaker. "You're the only person left. Everyone else has turned it down."

"I said I DON'T WANT IT," he replied. He added some extra oomph to his words that time.

Whittaker was right. Phil really did speak like leadership material. Of course, that's exactly what Phil didn't want to be.

Phil and Whittaker both lived in the village of Bottom. The people who lived there demanded a lot from their leader.

There were rumours that this was why Stephanie took a break from being leader. There were other rumours that Stephanie had taken more than a break all the way to the Philippines on the other side of the planet.

Nobody knew exactly what had happened to Stephanie, but Bottom needed a new leader.

Whittaker had asked Crazy Steve, Odd Nancy, Tattoo Stan, Tattoo Stan's nephew, Joseph the Wise (and his mum) and now Phil.

"I know who you can ask," said Phil.

Chapter Two:
The Last Hope

There was a loud knock. Nina didn't notice it. In fact, she probably didn't care. Nina's butler, Murphy, tapped her shoulder.

"There are people outside who want to talk to you," he said.

"Whatever," grunted Nina. Murphy was used to that word.

Whenever anybody asked her anything, she would snort back the word 'whatever'. Sometimes Murphy tricked her.

"Can I take the afternoon off work?" he would slip into conversation.

"Whatever!" Nina would grunt. Before she'd realised what she had said, Murphy would be gone.

Today wasn't the time for tricks. Bottom needed a hero. Whittaker stood by Nina's bed.

"Nina," whimpered Whittaker, "will you be Bottom's new leader?"

"Whatever," Nina mumbled.

"R-r-really?" stammered Whittaker.

"I SAID WHATEVER!" shouted Nina.

Chapter Three:
Funkytown

The next day, The Bottom Telegraph's headline read: 'Finding Nina: The search for a new leader is OVER'. Bottom's residents felt like they could relax again. Murphy didn't.

"Be careful, Nina. The people of Bottom are very demanding," Murphy warned her.

"Whatever," she said.

There was a knock at the door. It was Tattoo Stan. He had a question for Nina.

"Nina, now that you're the leader, do you think it would be alright for me to keep a pet dolphin?" he asked.

Murphy started his point. "See Nina, this is exactly what I mea-"

"Whatever," sighed Nina.

She was too busy playing on her phone to care.

Stan was happy. He skipped down the path, whistling a merry tune. Murphy slammed the door.

"Really? A pet dolphin?" ranted Murphy. "You must take care with decisions or Bottom will end up in a big mess!"

Knock, knock.

People were queuing. Each person asked Nina for a new rule. The problem was that Nina only answered questions one way...

Joseph the Wise asked Nina to make people greet each other by doing a handstand.

"Whatever..."

Odd Nancy wanted telephones banned. She wanted to replace them with megaphones.

"Whatever..."

Nina even let Crazy Steve and Tattoo Stan's new gorilla and white tiger stay.

Joseph's mum got a rule made where only dogs could drive cars.

Whittaker even got Nina to rename Bottom. Now it was called Funkytown.

Every time Nina said 'whatever', Funkytown got crazier.

Murphy pulled Nina over. "I warned you, Nina! When will you learn?" he whispered.

Nina didn't listen. For every person queuing, a new rule was made.

The streets of Funkytown were very funky indeed. Half of the villagers were greeting each other with handstands. The other half were shouting from building to building with megaphones.

Gorillas and white tigers were walking on the pavements, while poodles and pugs were driving on the roads.

'Whatever' had become the most dangerous phrase of all in Funkytown.

Chapter Four:
Nice One, Phil

Funkytown's new rules had gone down well. The dogs had even started a taxi company called K9 Cabs, where people paid in biscuits.

For one person, though, Funkytown wasn't quite funky enough. Phil hobbled his way up to Nina's house.

"We old folk can't keep up with all these rules!" Phil chuckled to Nina. "I think we should just have one rule," he said. A sinister smile grew on his face. "That one rule should be... that there are no rules!"

"Nina, wait!" Murphy yelled. "You cannot make this rule!"

Murphy pleaded with Nina. "If you make this rule, then I will leave. I won't watch my beautiful Bottom be turned into a lawless Funkytown," he blubbered.

"So, what's your decision? Can we make the rule?" asked Phil.

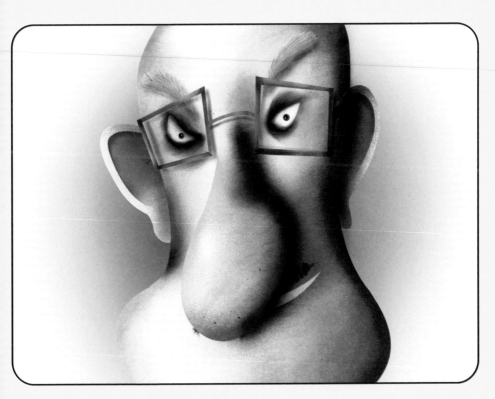

"Whatever," grunted Nina.

Murphy's heart sank. He grabbed his coat and walked off into the rain.

Phil, on the other hand, jumped to his feet. He ripped off his suit. Underneath, he had a vest, leather trousers and more tattoos than Stan. He put on a helmet and jumped on his motorcycle.

Before driving off into the chaos, Phil sneered back at Nina. "Just to let you know, Nina, having no rules means that you're no longer the leader of Funkytown!"

Nina finally said a new word.

"Whoops."

Chapter Five:
Give Me My Bottom Back!

One month later, Funkytown was a mess. K9 Cabs was now run by the gorilla and the white tiger, people worshipped saxophones and the only food left was whipped cream. In the middle of the madness, Nina was handing out pamphlets.

Nina had spent a month in the mayhem she had made. It helped her understand why she should have cared about the choices she made as leader. She was ready to turn Funkytown around, but she needed the help of an old friend.

Nina had decided to make a speech to the people of Funkytown.

"This village can be WHATEVER we want. It can be a Funkytown mess, or it can be a beautiful Bottom. I have five new rules I think we should follow if we all agree to. Who's with me?"

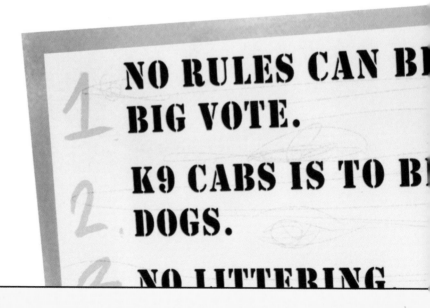

1. NO RULES CAN B[E] BIG VOTE.

2. K9 CABS IS TO B[E] DOGS.

3. NO LITTERING

The rules were:

1. No rules can be made without a big vote.
2. K9 Cabs is to be returned to the dogs.
3. No littering.
4. Phil must warn people before he rips off his suit.
5. Bottom shall never be renamed.

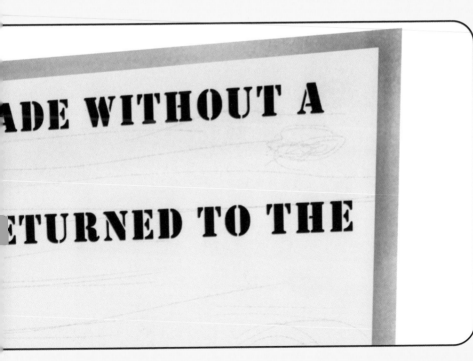

It took some time, but the village of Bottom was finally back to normal. Murphy forgave Nina after he heard her speech, but she still had one trick left.

"I have something to confess," Nina told Murphy. "I made a sixth rule..."

Nina opened the door to her bedroom. The gorilla was playing a saxophone, the dolphin was reading The Bottom Telegraph and the white tiger was napping.

"These guys don't have to leave. Can we keep them?" asked Nina.

"Whatever," giggled Murphy.

Rock Bottom: Quiz

1. Where was it rumoured that the previous leader Stephanie had run away to?

2. What pet did Tattoo Stan want to keep?

3. Why did Murphy walk off into the rain?

4. If you could make one rule for your town, village or city, what would it be?

5. How do you think Nina felt when she realised what she had done to Bottom?

Helpful Hints for Reading at Home

This 'really readable' Accessible Reader has been carefully written and designed to help children with learning differences whether they are reading in the classroom or at home. However, there are some extra ways in which you can help your child at home.

- Try to provide a quiet space for your child to read, with as few distractions as possible.

- Try to allow your child as much time as they need to decode the letters and words on the page.

- Reading with a learning difference can be frustrating and difficult. Try to let your child take short, managed breaks between reading sessions if they begin to feel frustrated.

- Build your child's confidence with positive praise and encouragement throughout.

- Your child's teacher, as well as many charities, can provide you with lots of tips and techniques to help your child read at home.